Robert Underwood Johnson

The Winter Hour

And Other Poems

Robert Underwood Johnson

The Winter Hour
And Other Poems

ISBN/EAN: 9783744714372

Printed in Europe, USA, Canada, Australia, Japan

Cover: Foto ©Thomas Meinert / pixelio.de

More available books at **www.hansebooks.com**

THE WINTER HOUR
AND OTHER POEMS

BY
ROBERT UNDERWOOD JOHNSON

NEW YORK
THE CENTURY CO.
1892

TO

RICHARD WATSON GILDER

.

CONTENTS

vii

THE WINTER HOUR AND OTHER POEMS

INVOCATION: TO THE GORSE

"When the gorse is out of bloom, then love is out of season."—
ENGLISH PROVERB.

HARDY gorse, that all year long
  Blooms upon the English moor,
  Let me set thee at the door
Of this little book of song.

When the dreary winter lowers,
  Vainly dost thou seek a fellow
  To thy blossom brave and yellow —
Color of the cheeriest flowers.

Thou of love perennial art
  Such a symbol that they say:
"When no gorse-bloom greets the day,
There 's no love in any heart."

1

INVOCATION

Thus all days are Love's and thine.—
  Spicy flower on thorny branch,
  In Love's service thou art stanch—
Wilt thou, wilding, enter mine?

THE WINTER HOUR

I

OF all the hours of day or night
Be mine the winter candle-light,
When Day's usurpers of Love's throne —
Fame, Pride, and tyrant Care — are flown,
And hearts are letters of hid desire
Yielding their secrets at the fire.
Now beauty in a woman's face
Glows with a sympathetic grace,
And friend draws closer unto friend,
Like travelers near a journey's end;
In casual talk some common hope
Finds fresher wing and farther scope;
The eye has language fit to speak
Thoughts that by day 't were vain to seek
Out of their silence; and the hand
Grasps with a comrade's sure demand.
Pile high the winter's cheer and higher, —
The world is saved, not lost, by fire!

HEARTH-SONG

WHEN November's night comes down
With a dark and sudden frown,
Like belated traveler chill
Hurrying o'er the tawny hill,—
　　Higher, higher
Heap the pine-cones in a pyre!
Where 's a warmer friend than fire?

Song 's but solace for a day;
Wine 's a traitor not to trust;
Love 's a kiss and then away;
Time 's a peddler deals in dust.
　　Higher, higher
Pile the driftwood in a pyre!
Where 's a firmer friend than fire?

Knowledge was but born to-night;
Wisdom 's to be born to-morrow;
One more log—and banish sorrow,
One more branch—the world is bright.
　　Higher, higher
Crown with balsam-boughs the pyre!
Where 's an older friend than fire?

II

O SILENT hour that sacred is
To our sincerest reveries!—
When peering Fancy fondly frames
Swift visions in the oak-leaved flames;
When Whim has magic to command
Largess and lore from every land,
And Memory, miser-like, once more
Counts over all her hoarded store.
Now phantom moments come again
In a long and lingering train,
As not content to be forgot —
(O Death! when I remember not
Such moments, may my current run,
Alph-like, to thy oblivion!):
The summer bedtime, when the sky —
The boy's first wonder — gathers nigh,
And cows are lowing at the bars,
And fireflies mock the early stars
That seem to hang just out of reach —
Like a bright thought that lacks of speech;
The wistful twilight's tender fall,
When to the trundle comes the call

Of fluting robins, mingling sweet
With voices down the village street;
The drowsy silence, pierced with fear
If evil-omened owl draw near,
Quaking with presage of the night;
The soft surrender when, from sight
Hid like a goddess in a cloud,
Comes furtive Sleep, with charm endowed
To waft the willing child away
Far from the margin of the day,
Till chanticleer with roystering blare
Of reveille proclaims the glare.
Remember?—how can one forget
(Since Memory 's but Affection's debt)
Those faëry nights that hold the far,
Soft rhythm of the low guitar,
When not more sweetly zephyr blows
And not more gently Afton flows
Than the dear mother's voice, to ease
The hurts of day with brook and breeze,
To soothing chords that haunt the strings
Like shadows of the song she sings!
And as the music's lullaby
Locks down at last the sleepy eye,

THE WINTER HOUR

Green visions of a distant hill
The fancy of the singer fill,
While spreads Potomac's pausing stream,
And moonlight sets her heart adream
Of that old time when love was made
With valentine and serenade.

Now, too, come bedtimes when the stair
Was never climbed alone.—Ah, where,
Beyond the midnight and the dawn,
Has now that other footstep gone?
Does sound or echo more reveal
When thirty winters may not steal
That still-returning tread,—that voice,
That made the timid child rejoice
Against the terrors of the wind,—
That tender tone that smoothed the mind?
Great heart of pity! it was then
God seemed a father, denizen
Of His own world, not chained to feet
Of some far, awful judgment-seat.
Then was revealed the reverent soul
Whom creed nor doubt could from the
    goal

Of goodness swerve; who need not bend
To be of each just cause the friend.
Of whose small purse and simple prayer
The neediest had the largest share;
Beloved of child, and poor, and slave,
Nor yet more lovable than brave;
Whom place could not allure, nor pelf,—
To all men generous save himself;
Whose passion Freedom was — with no
Heat-lightning rage devoid of blow,
But as a bridegroom might defend
His chosen, to the furious end.

Still other moments come apace,
Each with fond, familiar face:
The pleasures of an inland boy
To whom great Nature was a toy
For which all others were forsook —
A spirit blithesome as a brook
Whose song in ripples crystalline
Doth flow soft silences between;
The dormant soul's slow wakenings
To dimly-apprehended things;

THE WINTER HOUR

The sudden vision in the night
As by a conflagration's light;
The daily miracle of breath;
The awe of battle and of death;
The tears of grief at Sumter's gun,
The tears of joy when war was done,
And all the fainting doubt that masked
As hope when news of war was asked.
And oh! that best-remembered place,
That perfect moment's melting grace,—
The look, the smile, the touch, the kiss,
The halo of self-sacrifice,—
When Nature's passion, bounteous June,
To Love's surrender added boon,
As though the heir of every age
Had come into his heritage.

THE LOST ROSE

THERE was a garden sweet and gay,
Where rarest blossoms did delay
The look that Fanny bent to find
The flower fairest to her mind,
Till, at her word, I plucked for her
A rose of York-and-Lancaster.

The red did with the white agree,
Like passion blent in purity;
And as she blushed and blushed the more,
Till she was like the bloom she bore,
I said, "Dear heart, I too prefer
The rose of York-and-Lancaster."

'T is years ago and miles away!
For oh! nor rose nor maid could stay
To freshen other Junes. And yet
How few who do not quite forget! —
Or know to which the words refer:
"Sweet rose of York-and-Lancaster."

In vain, when roses do appear
Upon the bosom of the year,
I search the tangle and the town
Among the roses of renown,
And still the answer is—"Oh, sir,
We know no York-and-Lancaster."

But ah, my heart, it knows the truth,
And where was sown that seed of youth;
And though the world have lost the rose,
There 's still one garden where it grows—
Where every June it breathes of her,
My rose of York-and-Lancaster.

III

Now call the Muses' aid to flout
The bleak storm's roaring rage without;
And bring it hail, or bring it snow,
It shall be Love's delight to show
What Fire and two defenders dare
Against the legions of the air,
Whose sharpest arrows shall not find
Cleft in the armor of the mind.
Why dread we Winter's deep distress,
His pale and frigid loneliness,
When here at hand are stored, in nooks,
All climes, all company, in books!
A moving tale for every mood,
Shakspere for all,— the fount and food
Of gentle living,— Fancy's link
'Twixt what we are and what we think,—
Fellow to stars that nightly plod
Old Space, yet kindred to the clod.
Choose now from his world's wizard play
What is frolicsome and gay;
'T was for such evening he divined
Not Juliet but Rosalind.

Put the storied sorrow down,—
Not to-night, with Jove-like frown,
Shall the mighty Tuscan throw
Fateful lightnings at his foe,
Nor Hawthorne bend his graceful course
To follow motive to its source.
No, let gladness greet the ear:
Cervantes' wit, or Chaucer's cheer,
Or Lamb's rich cordial, pure and sweet,
Where aromatic tinctures meet;
Or princely Thackeray, whose pages
Yield humor wiser than the sages;
Or, set in cherished place apart,
Poets that keep the world in heart:
Milton's massive lines that pour
Like waves upon a windward shore;
Wordsworth's refuge from the crowd—
The peace of noon-day's poisèd cloud;
That flaming torch a jealous line
Passed on to Keats from Beauty's shrine;
Visions of Shelley's prophet-soul,
That, seeing part, could sing the whole,
Most like a lark that mounts so high
He sees not earth but from the sky.

And of the bards who in the grime
And turmoil of our changing time
Have kept the faith of men most pure
The three whose harps shall last endure :
Browning, Knight of Song,—so made
By Nature's royal accolade,—
Whose lines, as life-blood full and warm,
Search for the soul within the form,
And in the treasures of whose lore
Is Love, Love, ever at the core;
Tennyson, of the silver string,
Wisest of the true that sing,
And truest singer of the wise;
And he whose "stairway of surprise"
Soars to an outlook whence appear
All best things, fair, and sure, and near.

IV

Upon the wall some impress fine
Of Angelo's majestic line —
Seer or sibyl, dark with fate;
Near, and all irradiate,

Bellini's holy harmonies,
Bringing the gazer to his knees;
One group to hint from what a height
Titian with color dowers the sight;
A pageant of Carpaccio,
Flushed with an autumn sunset-glow;
Then, of Luini's pensive race,
The Columbine's alluring grace;
And, echo of an age remote,
Beato's pure and cloistered note.
And be not absent from the rest
Some later flame of beauty (blest
As a new star), lest it be said
That Art, that had its day, is dead.
Let Millet speak in melting tone —
Voicing the life that once was stone,
Ere Toil had found another dawn
Of Bethlehem at Barbizon.
Nor is it winter while Dupré
With daring sunlight leads the way
Into the woodland rich and dim;
Who love the forest, follow him;
And they who lean the ear to reach
The whispering breath of Nature's speech,

May with Daubigny wait the night
Beside a lake of lambent light
And margèd darkness — at the hour
(Soul of the evening!) when the power
Of man, that morn with empire shod,
Is shattered by a thought of God!
And ah, one more: we will not wait
For Death to let us call him great,
But, taking counsel of the heart
Stirred by his pure and perfect art,
Among the masters make a place
For Dagnan's fair Madonna's face.

A MADONNA OF DAGNAN-BOUVERET

OH, brooding thought of dread!
Oh, calm of coming grief!
Oh, mist of tears unshed
Above that shining head
That for an hour too brief
Lies on thy nurturing knee!
How shall we pity thee,
Mother of sorrows — sorrows yet to be!

That babyhood unknown
With all of bright or fair
That lingers in our own
By every hearth has shone.
Each year that light we share
As Bethlehem saw it shine.
Be ours the comfort thine,
Mother of consolations all divine!

V

NOR be the lesser arts forgot
On which Life feeds and knows it not,
That everywhere from roof to portal
. Beauty may speak of the immortal:
Forms that the fancy over-fill;
Colors that give the sense a thrill;
Soft lights that fall through opal glass
On mellow stuffs and sturdy brass;
Corners of secrecy that invite
Comfort, the handmaid of Delight;
The very breath of sculptures old
Held poised within a perfect mold;

A dainty vase of Venice make,
Fashioned for its one rose's sake
Ay, winter's miracle of flowers
To cheat the mood and mask the hours:
Love's velvet-petaled pledge of June,
That, on the wings of Passion strewn,
Made courtly Persia conqueror
Of thrice the world she lost in war; —
Jonquils, that Tuscan sunshine hold
Within their happy hearts of gold; —
Narcissus, such as still are found
By Marathon's mountain-envied mound —
Food of the soul, well bought with bread,
As sage Hippocrates hath said.
All these perchance shall faintly yield
Odors from some Sicilian field
Where young Theocritus deep-strayed
In blooms celestial — where his shade,
Haunting his storied Syracuse,
Finds balm for his neglected Muse.
Add wanton smilax to entwine
Your Dancing Faun or God of Wine,
And you shall summon in a band
The joys of every summer land.

2

VI

BUT there 's a vision stirs the heart
Deeper than books or flowers or art,—
When Music, mistress of the mind,
Lender not borrower from the Wind,
Rival of Water and of Light,
Adds her enchantment to the Night.
What thoughts! what dreams! what ecstasies
When heart and fingers touch the keys!
Across what gulf of fate Love springs
To Love, if Love caress the strings!
By this· mysterious amulet
One shall remember or forget;
When words and smiles and tears shall fail,
The might of Music shall prevail;
Shall move alike the wise and weak;
All dialects alike shall speak;
Outglow the rainbow to the doomed.—
Consuming all, be unconsumed;
Shall save a nation in its throes,
Luring with concord grappling foes;
Shall madden thus, yet shall be glad
(Oh, paradox!) to soothe the mad.

This rhythmic language made to reach
Beyond the reticence of speech —
Bland as the breeze of May it sighs,
Or rolls reverberant till the skies
Tremble with majesty! Not the mote
Most hid of all creation's rote
But holds some message that shall. be
Transmuted into harmony.
Already, since the lisping-time
When music was but chant or chime,
What spirits have to man been lent
From God's discordless firmament! —
Beethoven, brother of the Nine,
But with a birthright more divine, —
Whose harmonies that heavenward wend
Wings to the laden spirit lend
Until, serenely mounting higher,
It melts into the starry choir;
Wagner, in whom the Passions meet
To throw themselves at Music's feet, —
Whose murmurings have charm to wring
From Love the secret of the Spring, —
And in whose clamor sounds the siege
Of heaven when Lucifer was liege.

Händel, whose aspirations seem
Like steps of gold in Jacob's dream;
Mozart, simplest of the great,
Heir of Melody's estate,
Who did blithe pipes of Pan prolong
And heighten to a seraph song.
Schumann, rare poet, with a lyre
Stringed in Imagination's fire;
And oh, that one of human strain!—
Chopin, beloved child of pain,
To whom the whole of Love was known
Marvel, and mystery, and moan,
The joy secure, the jealous dart
Deep-ambushed in the doubting heart,
And all the perilous delight
That waits on doubt, as dawn on night.

Ah, who shall wake the charm that lies
Past what is written for the eyes
In such a scroll? The poet's need
Is that a poet's heart should read.
Happy the winter hour and fleet
When flame and waiting passion meet

In her pure fire whose chords betray
The St. Cecilia of our day!
Oh, velvet of that Saxon hand
So lately iron to command!—
Like, at the shower's sudden stop,
The softness of the clinging drop.
What tender notes the trance prolóng
Of that famed rhythmic cradle-song!
How faëry is her woven spell
Of minuet or tarantelle!
Who would return to earth when she
Transports us with a rhapsody!
And when in some symphonic burst
Of joy her spirit is immersed,
That path celestial fain to share,
We vow to breathe but noble air!

VII

WARMED with melody like wine,
Lighted by the friendly shine
Of the rich-replenished hearth,
Let us drink of wine and mirth

While waning evening's aftermath
Grows pleasant as a winding path
With wit's surprises and the tale
Adventurous, spreading sudden sail
For Arcady and hallowed haunts
Along the shores of old Romance:
Now shall fare the fancy forth
To pillared grottoes of the north,
Where circling waters come again
Like thoughts within a sleepless brain;
Or, coursing down a softer coast
Whose beauty is the Old World's boast,
Shall pause for words while memory's flame
Kindles at Taormina's name.

And now in shifting talk appears
Pomp of cities clad with years:
Gay or gloomy with her skies,
Gray Paris like an opal lies
Sparkling on the front of France.
Avignon doth hold a lance
In a tourney-list with Nîmes.
Fair Seville basks in helpless dream

Of conquest, as in cagèd air
Dreams the tamed lion of his lair.
Regal Genoa still adorns
Her ancient throne; and Pisa mourns.
Now we traverse holy ground
Where three miracles are found:
One of beauty — when with dyes
Of her own sunset Venice vies.
One of beauty and of power —
Rome, the crumbled Babel-tower
Of centuries piled on centuries —
Scant refuge from Oblivion's seas
That swept about her. And the third? —
O heart, fly homeward like a bird,
And look, from Bellosguardo's goal,
Upon a city with a soul!
Who that has climbed that heavenly
        height
When all the west was gold with light,
And nightingales adown the slope
To listening Love were lending hope,
Till they by vesper bells were drowned,
As though by censers filled with sound —

Who — who would wish a worthier end
To every journey? or not blend
With those who reverently count
This their Transfiguration Mount?

LOVE IN ITALY

THEY halted at the terrace wall;
  Below, the towered city lay;
The valley in the moonlight's thrall
  Was silent in a swoon of May.
As hand to hand spoke one soft word
  Beneath the friendly ilex-tree,
They knew not, of the flame that stirred,
  What part was Love, what Italy.

They knew what makes the moon more bright
  Where Beatrice and Juliet are, —
The sweeter perfume in the night,
  The lovelier starlight in the star;
And more that glowing hour did prove,
  Beneath the sheltering ilex-tree, —
That Italy transfigures Love,
  As Love transfigures Italy.

VIII

AND thou, who art my winter hour—
Book, picture, music, friend, and flower—
If on such evening, dear, I trace
Paths far from Love's divine embrace,
Wandering till long absence grows
Into brief death—less death's repose—
Let me be missed with love and cheer,
As miss we those of yesteryear
With whom we thought (beguiling hope!)
To stray together down Life's slope,
While Age came on like gentle rain.
They who but ceased their joyous strain—
Where may the limit to the sea
Of their bereaving silence be?
Yet sorrow not: we may prolong,
If not the singer's voice, the song.
And if beyond the glorious strife
Of this good world, I tread new life,
Reluctant, but, by Heaven's aid,
With infant instinct unafraid,

May Memory plead with thee to save
Out of my song its happier stave.
From the Dark Isthmus let not gloom
Deepen the shadows of thy room.
For me no ban of smile or jest:
Life at its full is holiest.
Let all thy days have pure employ
In the high sanity of joy;
Be then, as now, the friend of all,
Thy heart a thronged confessional,
A fount of sympathy, a store
Of jewels at an open door.

Here do I falter, love, for fear
Of sacrilege to what is dear.
Not now—not here; some luminous time,
Some perfect place, some fortunate rhyme
May yield that sacrificial part
That poets fitly give to Art.
Ever the moment most elate
Must for a speech sufficient wait;
Only the happiest know, alas!
How soundless is the brimming glass.

But, though Love need not praise nor oath,
And silence oft is firmer troth,
Yet know that if I come no more,
'Tis fault of sail, or sea, or shore,
Not of the pilot,— for the heart
Sees its way homeward from the start.
If Death have bond that Love can break,
It shall be broken for thy sake.
If spirits unto mortals teach
Some rudiment of subtler speech,
My presence shall about thee stay
To prompt the word it cannot say.

So when, with late farewell and slow,
The guests into the night shall go,
Each pulse by sympathy more warm,
Forgetting the forgotten storm,
And thou alone into the blaze,
Thrilled with the best of life, shalt gaze
With hunger for the life divine,
Oh, be that blessed moment mine!—
With thee, who art my winter hour,
Book, picture, music, friend, and flower.

A SPRING PRELUDE

O TARDY April, is thy full choir here?
The redbreast, picket of the swarming spring,
Whistles a sudden chirrup of alarm
Before his level flight; and soft at eve
His melody, on grass half-robin high,
Falls like a vesper's throbbings from aloft.
The sparrow tempts the turf to faster growth
With her coy nesting, while her happy mate,
High in the promise-reddened maple-top,
O'er-bubbles with ecstasies of hoarded song.
The mellow tunings of the oriole's flute,
Rich as his coat, foretell his summer joy
And pitch the key of gladness for the year.
Here is the bluebird, best of mates and sires,
And pewee, restless as a lover's fear,
With cousin phœbe, bleating tearfully.
The humblebee, that, nectar-drunk, shall soon
Linger within the sybaritic flower,

Feeds his impatience at the cautious bud;
And from the furrows' wet and windy reach,
Where March but lately swung his icy scythe,
Ripples the velvet air about the cheek,
Laden with faintest chorusings, as though
The brimming silence overflowed in sound.

O tardy April, is the full choir here?
Alas for me! thou hast forgot to bring
Out of the South one childish, bird-like voice,
Whose absence doth delay the year, and makes
My songs and thine but preludes till she comes.

BEFORE THE BLOSSOM

In the tassel-time of spring
Love 's the only song to sing;
  Ere the ranks of solid shade
Hide the bluebird's flitting wing,
  While in open forest glade
No mysterious sound or thing
  Haunt of green has found or made,
Love 's the only song to sing.

Though in May each bush be dressed
Like a bride, and every nest
  Learn Love's joyous repetend,
Yet the half-told tale is best
  At the budding,— with its end
Much too secret to be guessed,
  And its fancies that attend
April's passion unexpressed.

Love and Nature communing
Gave us Arcady. Still ring —
　Vales across and groves among —
Wistful memories, echoing
　Pan's far-off and fluty song.
Poet! nothing harsher sing;
　Be, like Love and Nature, young
In the tassel-time of spring.

LOVE IN THE CALENDAR

WHEN chinks in April's windy dome
    Let through a day of June,
And foot and thought incline to roam,
    And every sound 's a tune;
When Nature fills a fuller cup,
    And hides with green the gray,—
Then, lover, pluck your courage up
    To try your fate in May.

Though proud she was as sunset clad
    In Autumn's fruity shades,
Love too is proud, and brings (gay lad!)
    Humility to maids.
Scorn not from nature's mood to learn,
    Take counsel of the day:
Since haughty skies to tender turn,
    Go try your fate in May.

Though cold she seemed as pearly light
   Adown December eves,
And stern as night when March winds smite
   The beech's lingering leaves;
Yet Love hath seasons like the year,
   And grave will turn to gay,—
Then, lover, harken not to fear,
   But try your fate in May.

And you whose art it is to hide
   The constant love you feel:
Beware, lest overmuch of pride
   Your happiness shall steal.
No longer pout, for May is here,
   And hearts will have their way;
Love 's in the calendar, my dear,
   So yield to fate in May.

A SEPTEMBER VIOLET

For days the peaks wore hoods of cloud,
  The slopes were veiled in chilly rain;
We said: It is the Summer's shroud,
And with the brooks we moaned aloud,—
  Will sunshine never come again?

At last the west wind brought us one
  Serene, warm, cloudless, crystal day,
As though September, having blown
A blast of tempest, now had thrown
  A gauntlet to the favored May.

Backward to Spring our fancies flew,
  And, careless of the course of Time,
The bloomy days began anew.
Then, as a happy dream comes true,
  Or as a poet finds his rhyme,—

Half wondered at, half unbelieved,—
   I found thee, friendliest of the flowers!
Then Summer's joys came back, green-leaved,
And its doomed dead, awhile reprieved,
   First learned how truly they were ours.

Dear violet! Did the Autumn bring
   Thee vernal dreams, till thou, like me,
Didst climb to thy imagining?
Or was it that the thoughtful Spring
   Did come again, in search of thee?

SEPTEMBER'S EVE

I

'T is Nature's temple, and the day
Is full of worship as of light.
A sigh from now and 't will be night;
The lordly vision will not stay.
With dusky incense throbs the gray
Half dome of sky. A cloistered note
Of lingering bird-song sounds remote
As the last echo of a hymn
Sung in recessional, cold and dim.
I worship, but as though the praise
Must pass through Nature's priestly ways,
For God doth seem as lone and far
As yonder uncompanioned star,
                    September's Eve.

II

ALONG the mountain's altar-crest
The russet deepens in the West,
As when to richer chords the close
Of noble music softly flows.
Now speed my footsteps through the dark,
I see my leaping hearth, and hark!
Th' expectant children's view-halloo
Rings out a melody of cheer.
The rushing feet approach; I hear
The lavish welcome panting through.
How bright the sudden stars appear
In friendly groups! Now God is near,
For Love is in *her* temple, too,
                September's Eve.

OCTOBER

Soft days whose silver moments keep
The constant promise of the morn,
When tired equinoctials sleep,
And wintry winds are yet unborn:
What one of all the twelve more dear—
Thou truce and Sabbath of the year?

More restful art thou than the May,
And if less hope be in thy hand,
Some cares 't were grief to understand
Thou hid'st, as is the mother's way,
With mists and lights of fairy-land
Set on the borders of the day.

And best of all thou dost beguile
With color,— friendliest thought of God!
Than thine hath heaven itself a smile
More rich? Are feet of angels shod
With peace more fair? O month divine!
Stay, till thy tranquil soul be mine.

IN NOVEMBER

HERE is the watershed of all the year,
Where, by a thought's space, thoughts do start anear
That fare most widely forth: some to the mouth
Of Arctic rivers, some to the mellow South.

The gaunt and wrinkled orchard shivers 'neath
The blast, like Lear upon the English heath,
And mossy boughs blow wild that, undistressed,
Another spring shall hide the cheerful nest.

All things are nearer from this chilly crown,—
The solitude, the white and huddling town;
And next the russet fields, of harvest shorn,
Shines the new wheat that freshens all the morn.

From out the bursting milkweed, dry and gray,
The silken argosies are launched away,
To mount the gust, or drift from hill to hill
And plant new colonies by road and rill.

Ah, wife of mine, whose clinging hand I hold,
Shrink you before the New, or at the Old?
And those far eyes that hold the silence fast—
Look they upon the Future, or the Past?

ON NEARING WASHINGTON

CITY of homes and in my heart my home!
  (Though other streets exact a grudging fee):
  How leap my pulses when afar I see
  The dawn creep whitening down thy solemn dome!
For now my care-restricted steps may roam
  Thy urban groves — a forest soon to be —
  Where, like thy shining river, placid, free,
  Contentment dwells and beckons me to come.

Ah, city dear to lovers! — that dost keep
  For their delight what Mays and what Novem-
    bers! —
  Kindling the flame, and if it ever sleep,
New-lighting it within the breathing embers;
  Dear even in their sorrow! for when they weep
  'T is for rare joys, scarce known till Love remem-
    bers.

"AS A BELL IN A CHIME"

As a bell in a chime
　　Sets its twin-note a-ringing,
As one poet's rhyme
　　Wakes another to singing,
So, once she has smiled,
All your thoughts are beguiled
And flowers and song from your childhood are bringing.

Though moving through sorrow
　　As the star through the night,
She needs not to borrow,
　　She lavishes, light.
The path of yon star
Seemeth dark but afar:
Like hers it is sure, and like hers it is bright.

Each grace is a jewel
   Would ransom the town,
Her speech has no cruel,
   Her praise is renown;
'T is in her as though Beauty,
Resigning to Duty
The scepter, had still kept the purple and crown.

IN THE DARK

AT dusk, when Slumber's gentle wand
   Beckons to quiet fields my boy,
And day, whose welcome was so fond,
   Is slighted like a rivaled toy,—

When fain to follow, fain to stay,
   Toward night's dim border-line he peers,
We say he fears the fading day:
   Is it the inner dark he fears?

His deep eyes, made for wonder, keep
   Their gaze upon some land unknown,
The while the crowding questions leap
   That show his ignorance my own.

For he would go he knows not where,
   And I—I hardly know the more;
Yet what is dark and what is fair
   He would to-night with me explore.

Upon the shoals of my poor creed
  His plummet falls, but cannot rest;
To sound the soundless is his need,
  To find the primal soul his quest.

In vain these bird-like flutterings,
  As when through cages sighs the wind:
My clearest answer only brings
  New depths of mystery to his mind,—

Vague thoughts, by crude surmise beset,
  And groping doubts that loom and pass
Like April clouds that, shifting, fret
  With tides of shade the sun-wooed grass.

O lonely soul within the crowd
  Of souls! O language-seeking cry!
How black were noon without a cloud
  To vision only of the eye!

Sleep, child! while healing Nature breaks
  Her ointment on the wounds of Thought;
Joy, that anew with morning wakes,
  Shall bring you sight it ne'er has brought.

Lord, if there be, as wise men spake,
　No Death, but only Fear of Death,
And when Thy temple seems to shake
　'T is but the shaking of our breath,—

Whether by day or night we see
　Clouds where Thy winds have driven none,
Let unto us as unto Thee
　The darkness and the light be one.

GOOD MEASURE OF LOVE

ONE twilight was there when it seemed
New stars beneath young eyelids gleamed;

In vain the warning clock would creep
Anear the hour of beauty-sleep.

In vain the trundle yearned to hold
Far-Eyes and little Heart-of-Gold;

And love that kisses are the stuff of
At last for once there was enough of,

As though of all Affection's round
The fond climacteric had been found —

Each childish fancy heaping more,
Like spendthrift from a miser-store,

Till stopped by hug and stayed by kiss —
The sweet contention ran like this:

" How much do I love you ? " (I remember but
    Of the words of the troth of this lover)
" I love you "—he said—" why—I love you—a
    Brimful and running over.

" I love you a hundred!" said he, with a squee;
    " A thousand!" said she, as she nestled;
" A million!" he cried in triumphant ease
    While she with the numbers wrestled.

"Aha! I have found it!" she shouted, "aha!"
    (The red to the soft cheeks mounting)
" I love you — I love you — I love you, Papa,
    Over the last of the counting!"

NOBLESSE OBLIGE

WHAT is diviner than the peace of foes!
    He conquers not who does not conquer hate,
    Or thinks the shining wheels of heaven wait
    On his forgiving. Dimmer the laurel shows
On brows that darken; and war-won repose
    Is but a truce when heroes abdicate
    To Huns — unfabling those of elder date
Whose every corse a fiercer warrior rose.

O ye that saved the land! Ah yes, and ye
    That mourned its saving! Neither need forget
    The price our destiny did of both demand —
Toil, want, wounds, prison, and the lonely sea
    Of tears at home. Oh, look on these. And yet —
    Before the human fail you—quick! your hand!

4

ON A CANDIDATE ACCUSED OF YOUTH

"Too young" do they call him? Who say it? Not they
Who have felt his hard stroke in the civic affray,
When elders, whom veteran fighters had taught
Till they knew all the rules by which battles are fought,
Fumbled weakly with weapons his foresight had sought.

Who thinks of his youthfulness? Surely not they
Who stood at his side through the wavering day,
And knew the quick vision, the planning exact
Of parry and thrust, till the stout helmet cracked
'Neath the bold and true blow that is better than tact.

Yea, the strength of the arm is the strength of its use,
Not its years; and when fighting is on, better choose
Not the rust-eaten sword from the library wall,
But the new blade that leaps in its sheath at the call.
Ask the foe by which weapon he fears most to fall!

WASHINGTON HYMN

SUNG AT THE LAYING OF THE CORNER-STONE OF THE
WASHINGTON MEMORIAL ARCH, NEW YORK, MAY
30, 1890, TO THE AIR OF THE AUSTRIAN
HYMN BY HAYDN

PRAISE to Thee, O God of Freedom,
    Praise to Thee, O God of Law,
Thee the goal of Israel's dreaming,
    Thee the flame that Moses saw;
Light of every patriot dungeon,
    Home of exile, hope of slave,
Loved by just and feared by tyrant,
    Comrade of the true and brave.

Would we pray for new defenders,
    Thou art with us ere we call;
Thou wilt find new ranks of heroes
    For the heroes yet to fall.

Back we look across the ages,
Forward Thou beyond the sun,
Yet no greater gift we ask Thee
Than another Washington.

TO RALPH WALDO EMERSON

ON THE DEATH OF GARFIELD, SEPTEMBER, 1881

POET of every soul that grieves
 O'er death untimely: whose lament
Lights up the farthest Dark, and leaves
 A bow across the heavens bent:

Dead in an upper room doth lie
 A nation's hero; can it be
Thy ear too faintly hears the cry
 The West wind utters to the sea?

Thy Concord pæan may have caught
 Glow from an elder Garfield's name:
What fitter aureole could be sought
 For such a son than such a flame!

Bard of the Human: since we yearn
  For that one manly heart in vain,
Forgive the reverent eyes that turn
  Toward the low stream in Concord plain.

Warned by the favoring touch of Death,
  Thy *Nunc Dimittis* thou hast sung;
No more the thunder's stormy breath
  Shall sweep the lyre with lightnings strung.

And yet, for him, remains—unsigned,
  Unspoken—all thy noble praise,
When (port more worth the cruise!) thou find
  His sail beyond the final haze;

But us? . . . . . O Seer, to whose gift
  Looms large the Future's better part,
What other prophet voice shall lift
  This burden from the people's heart!

ILLUSIONS

Go stand at night upon an ocean craft,
And watch the folds of its imperial train
Catching in fleecy foam a thousand glows —
A miracle of fire unquenched by sea.
There in bewildering turbulence of change
Whirls the whole firmament, till as you gaze,
All else unseen, it is as heaven itself
Had lost its poise, and each unanchored star
In phantom haste flees to the horizon line.

What dupes we are of the deceiving eye!
How many a light men wonderingly acclaim
Is but the phosphor of the path Life makes
With its own motion, while above, forgot,
Sweep on serene the old unenvious stars!

TO-MORROW

ONE walks secure in wisdom-trodden ways
That lead to peaceful nights through happy days —
Health, fame, friends, children, and a gentle wife,
All Youth can covet or Experience praise,
And Use withal to crown the ease of life.
    Ah, thirsting for another day,
        How dread the fear
    If he but knew the danger near!

Another, with some old inheritance
Of Fate, unmitigated yet by Chance,—
Condemned by those he loves, with no appeal
To his own fearful heart, that ever pants
For newer circlings of the cruel Wheel!
    Ah, thirsting for another day,
        What need of fear
    If he but knew the help that 's near?

INSCRIPTION FOR A BURIAL URN

FIRE is older than Earth,
Swaddled her at her birth,
Shall be her windy shroud.
Fear whispers, *Earth with fire endowed*
Is all of Life : but the Soul's Desire
Is something other than earth and fire,
And cannot mold or burn.
Of this is Honor made, and Truth,
And Love that shall out-light the star.
Go find when these began their youth,
Then guess their age's farthest bar ;
But look not for it in grave or urn.

QUALITY

I

TAKE, ere the bee hath sipped,
The courtly, maiden-lipped,
And dewy oleander,
And breathe, and dream, and wander.
But ah! take not another,
Lest fragrance fragrance smother.

II

What all your wreathèd wine
To what I taste of mine?
See the spilled jewels run,
Red as an autumn sun!—
Each holding warm and clear
The vintage of a year.

III

Stranger, thy passing word
My waiting heart hath stirred;
My life to thee I lend!
This hour thou art my friend,
And could not dearer be
Loved an eternity.

LUCK AND WORK

WHILE one will search the season over
To find the magic four-leaved clover,
Another, with not half the trouble,
Will plant a crop to bear him double.

ON A GREAT POET'S OBSCURITY

WHAT means his line? You say none knows?
 Yet one perhaps may learn — in time:
For, sure, could Life be told in prose
 There were no need at all for rhyme.

Alike two waters blunt the sight —
 The muddy shallow and the sea;
Here every current leads aright
 To deeps where lucent wonders be.

WRITTEN IN EMERSON'S POEMS

(FOR A CHILD)

MIDNIGHT or morning, eve or noon,
Torn March or clover-scented June,—
    Whene'er you stand before this gate,
'T will open — if but not too soon
    You knock, if only not too late.

Well shall it be if, boyhood gone,
A boy's delight you still may own
    To play the dawn-new game of life,—
If what is dreamed and what is known
    In your still-startled heart have strife.

Ere you have banished Mystery,
Or throned Distrust, or less shall be
    Stirred by the deep and fervent line
Which is the poet's sign and fee:
    Be this your joy that now is mine.

When comes the hour, be full and bright
Your lamp, as the wiser virgins' light!
  Choose some familiar, shrine-like nook,
And offer up in prayer the night
  Upon the altar of this book.

Always new earth, new heavens lie
The apocalyptic spirit nigh:
  If such be yours, oh, while you can,
Bid unregretted Youth good-bye,
  For morning shall proclaim you Man.

AMIEL

(THE "JOURNAL INTIME")

A FEW there are who to the troubled soul
Can lay the ear with that physician-art
Which by a whispered accent in the heart
Follows the lurking treason that hath stole
Into the citadel;—a few whose scroll
Of warning bears our safety,—is a chart
Of our unsounded seas, and doth impart
Courage to hold the spirit to its goal.

Of such is Amiel, lonely as a saint,—
Or as an eagle dwelling on peaks, in shade
Of clouds, which now he cleaves for one wide look
At the green earth, now for a circle faint
Nearer the sun. Once more has Truth betrayed
Secrets to Sorrow not in the sibyl's book.

"THE GUEST OF THE EVENING"

(READ AT THE DINNER TO RICHARD WATSON GILDER,
ON HIS BIRTHDAY FEBRUARY 8, 1884)

GOOD actions are a fruit so ripe and rare
They bear not fingering. Let me then beware
To touch with venturous hand this curving branch,
Nor lean too heedlessly against the tree
Thus, at its prime, o'erladen heavily
With golden harvest full and sweet and stanch,—
Lest I by some rude shock, at this light hour,
Bring down the Virtues in a mellow shower.

To drop the figure, friends,—let 's be content
The guest shall fancy less than we have meant;
Speak not too closely of his special good,
That we are here tells more than trumpets could.
Our friendship holds his virtues as the light
Holds the hid rainbow—storm but makes them bright;
The modest veil they wear I may not raise
Lest he should blush to hear, and I to praise.

5

SALVINI

DEAD is old Greece," they mourned ere yet arose
  This Greek—this oak of old Achaian graft
  Seed-sown where westward tempests wept and
      laughed,
As now when some great gust of heaven blows
From lair levantine. How the giant grows!—
  Not to lone ruin of a withered shaft,
  But quaffing life in every leafy draught,—
Fathered by Storm and mothered by Repose.

Nay, doubt the Greeks are gone till, this green
      crest
  In splendor fallen, round the wrack shall be
  Prolonged, like memories of a noble guest,
The phantom glory of the actor's day.
  Then, musing on Olympus, men shall say
  The myth of Jove took rise from lesser majesty.

FOR TEARS

SOME birches from the winter snow unbend,
   And some lie prone the happy summer long:
Is grief but weakness? May it be, blithe friend,
   The heavier burden stays but on the strong?

APPREHENSIONS

SEVEN days we sought the horizon line, elate,
   Without a sea-born doubt of things to come;
   Then on the eighth, upon the sill of home,
A fog, not of the sea, fell with a weight
Upon our spirits. Where was noon's rich freight
   Of summer cheer, the darkness spoke of doom,
   Till thoughts familiar did such dole assume
We could but cling before the coming fate.

In port—what greeting? From belovèd lips
   The same "All 's well!" that could not charr
      our woe
   Chanted an ocean litany against harm;
Our happiness swung forth from fear's eclipse.
   Alas! upon a fearless friend the blow
   Fell like first lightning from long-gathered storm

BROWNING AT ASOLO

(INSCRIBED TO HIS FRIEND MRS. ARTHUR BRONSON)

THIS is the loggia Browning lŏved,
 High on the flank of the friendly town;
These are the hills that his keen eye roved,
 The green like a cataract leaping down
  To the plain that his pen gave new renown.

There to the West what a range of blue!—
The very background Titian drew
 To his peerless Loves. O tranquil scene!
Who than thy poet fondlier knew
 The peaks and the shore and the lore between?

See! yonder 's his Venice—the valiant Spire,
 Highest one of the perfect three,
Guarding the others: the Palace choir,
The Temple flashing with opal fire—
 Bubble and foam of the sunlit sea.

Yesterday he was part of it all—
    Sat here, discerning cloud from snow
    In the flush of the Alpine afterglow,
    Or mused on the vineyard whose wine-stirred row
Meets in a leafy bacchanal.

Listen a moment—how oft did he!—
    To the bells from Fontalto's distant tower
Leading the evening in . . . ah, me!
Here breathes the whole soul of Italy
    As one rose breathes with the breath of the bower

Sighs were meant for an hour like this
    When joy is keen as a thrust of pain.
Do you wonder the poet's heart should miss
This touch of rapture in Nature's kiss
    And dream of Asolo ever again?

" Part of it yesterday," we moan?
    Nay, he is part of it now, no fear.
What most we love we are that alone.
His body lies under the Minster stone,
    But the love of the warm heart lingers here.

"LA MURA," ASOLO, June 3, 1892.

AT SEA

SOME things are undivined except by love—
Vague to the mind, but real to the heart,
As is the point of yon horizon line
Nearest the dear one on a foreign shore.

MOODS OF THE SOUL

I.— In Time of Victory

As soldiers after fight confess
　　The fear their valor would not own
When, ere the battle's thunder stress,
　　The silence made its mightier moan:

Though now the victory be mine,
　　'T is of the conflict I must speak,
Still wondering how the Hand Divine
　　Confounds the mighty with the weak.

To-morrow I may flaunt the foe—
　　Not now; for in the echoing beat
Of fleeing heart-throbs well I know
　　The bitterness of near defeat.

O friends! who see but steadfast deeds,
　　Have grace of pity with your praise.
Crown if you must, but crown with weeds,—
　　The conquered more deserve your bays.

No, praise the dead!—the ancestral roll
   That down their line new courage send,
For moments when against the soul
   All hell and half of heaven contend.

II.—In Time of Defeat

Yes, here is undisguised defeat—
   You say, " No further fight to lose."
With colors in the dust, 't is meet
   That tears should flow and looks accuse.

I echo every word of ruth
   Or blame: yet have I lost the right
To praise with you the unfaltering Truth,
   Whose power—save in me—has might?

Another day, another man:
   I am not *now* what I have been;
Each grain that through the hour-glass ran
   Rescued the sinner from his sin.

The Future is my constant friend;
  Above all children born to her
Alike her rich affections bend—
  She, the unchiding comforter.

Perhaps on her unsullied scroll
  (Who knows?) there may be writ at last
A fairer record of the soul
  For this dark blot upon the Past.

TO LEONORA

(AT HER DÉBUT, OCTOBER 18, 1891)

FAIR sister of the Muses, 't is the hour,
  Dearest of all, when thou dóst wed thy Art.
  No bride more radiant a more single heart
  Gave to her chosen — and what noble dower!
Graces akin to forest and to flower;
  A spirit blithe as dawn; a soul astart;
  A nature rich, to keep thee what thou art —
  A star of beauty and a flame of power.

Now, while the trancèd throng turn each to each
  Sharing their joy, think'st thou on those young years
  When many a day and night was unbeguiled
Save by this love that lightened toil and tears?
  Thy music melts upon the verge of speech;
  Fame greets the artist — I, the constant child.

HERBERT MAPES

(DROWNED AUGUST 23, 1891)

LAST night, what kingdom on his brow!
  What mellow music in his voice!
  What strength to make the eye rejoice!
What life! what flush of youth! . . . and now!

O brow dethroned! O muffled bell
  Of speech! O net too loosely wove!
  O sunken freight of hope and love!
Come back till we have said farewell!

A WISH FOR NEW FRANCE

(FRAGMENT)

FOR her no backward look
Into the bloody book
   Of kings. Thrice-rescued land!
Her haunted graves bespeak
A nobler fate : to seek
In service of the world again the world's command.

She, in whose skies of peace
Arise new auguries
   To strengthen, cheer, and guide —
When nations in a horde
Draw the unhallowed sword,
O Memory, walk a warning specter at her side!

DIVIDED HONORS *

NATURE had late a strife with Art
To prove which bears the worthier part
In poets' fame.　The words ran high
While Justice, friend to both, stood by
To name the victor.

　　　　　　　　Nature rose,
Impressive in her artless pose,
And in a few words fitly chose
(Confined to generalities)
Pleaded the *nature* of the thing —
That singers born to sing *must sing*,
That it could not be otherwise;
Spoke of the poet's " flight of wing,"
His " flow of song," his " zephyr sighs,"
And hid in trope and allegory
A whole campaign of *a priori.*

Then Art began to plead *her* cause;
Said Nature's windy words had flaws —

---

* Written for the dinner to James Whitcomb Riley at Indiana-
polis, October 18, 1888.

That e'en the larklet soaring high
Must surely once have *learned* to fly
And eke to sing. Moreover, Song
Is something more than baby-prattle;
Or plow-boy's carol to the cattle;
Or love's acrostic — though it be
Faultless (at one extremity);
Or verse that school-girls spoil a day for,
Found good to print, but not to pay for.
This well she with herself debated,
And, lacking points, elaborated,
And, like a lawyer closely pressed,
Naught having proved, assumed the rest.

But Justice, knowing how to prick
The airy globes of rhetoric,
Said, " Friends, your theories are ample,
Yet light upon the case we need,
And, *me judice*, she 'll succeed
Who shall present the best example."

A moment both were still as death,
Then shouted " Shakespeare!" in a breath;

And then, confounded by each other
(While pondering moderated pother),
Ran down the list of English charmers,
As in a fugue of two performers:
'T was "Chaucer!" "Philip Sidney!" "Donne!
"George Herbert!" "Milton!" "Tennyson!"
And, quick as either one would name them,
The other would be sure to claim them!—
Till Justice—blindfold all these years
Because she can't believe her eyes—
Convinced that hearing, too, belies,
Now pulled her bandage o'er her ears.
Then Nature, in affected candor,
Renounced all ownership in Landor,
And said: "Let 's both make fair returns;
I 'll give you Keats—you give me Burns."
"No, no," said Art, "you *have* a fit man,—
Your whole contention lies in Whitman."
Then, she not wanting from her rival
A gift of what was hers by right,
At once there followed a revival
Of acrimony—till in fright
Pale Justice, with a sly suggestion
Of dining, moved the previous question.

But Nature, conscious of her force,
Had in reserve a shrewd resource,
And, while the judgment hung uncertain,
She quickly drew aside a curtain,
And, full of confidence, said dryly:
" I rest my case on Whitcomb Riley!
And further to enforce my right,
He has consented to recite,
That all may see by how large part
He has possession of my heart."

.   .   .   .

Five minutes! and the wager 's o'er:
A ballad, homely, simple, true —
And then, and ever after, you
See Nature as you 'd ne'er before.
First is the kind eye's twinkling ray
So lit with human sympathy
That, kindled by its flash, you say
Humor 's the true democracy.
The next note 's deeper—there 's no guile
Mixed with the shrewdness of that smile
That breaks from sadness into joy—
The man's glad memory of the boy.

Then tears, ah! they are Nature's rain,
The tears of love and death and grief
And rapture—the divine relief
That gives us back the sun again.

.   .   .   .

No more need Nature nurse her fears,
For look! e'en Art herself 's in tears,
And in the general acclaim
The jade has nigh forgot her name.
Yet has she left one arrow more,
And, proudly rising to the floor,
" Not yet," she says, " for what you take
For Nature's work is mine, who make
Jewels of stones that else would lie
Unnoticed 'neath the searching sky.
Receive the secret—mine your tears:
He 's been my pupil fifteen years! "

Then Justice said: " Since there 's no winn
'T is fair the two should pay a dinner;
Nature shall furnish, Art prepare it,
And Riley, and his friends, shall share it."

A TRACER FOR J** B******

I

DEAR ENGLISH COUSINS: We have lost—
And crave your help to find him—
A farmer-poet, ocean-tossed,
With no address behind him.

Yes, though of song he write no stave,
We yet will call him poet:
His lines, as wave with following wave,
Make rhythm and never know it.

His pages grow rare fruits of thought,
Rare fruits of toil his furrows;
His name? Why hide it when you 've caught
The rhyme I seek?—John Burroughs.

I doubt if in the London round
His eager feet will loiter,
While hedge and copse of Kentish ground
Are left to reconnoiter.

There he 'll compare, in lulls of rain,
　　Your thrushes with our cat-bird,
And quiz the lads in every lane
　　For news of this or that bird.

Him leaners over Stratford gates
　　Shall mark, by Avon strolling.
A poacher? Ay, but on estates
　　Not near their vision rolling.

When Shakespeare tribute he has brought
　　Across the loyal ocean,
He 'll seek some haunt that Wordsworth sough
　　To pay his next devotion.

His " next "—ah! rather say his *first*,
　　Since friend is more than sovereign;
Of poets be the truth rehearsed:
　　To reign is not to govern.

To him the moor shall not be lone,
　　Nor any footstep idle
Where Nature hoards each lingering tone
　　Of the human voice of Rydal.

By poets led, he will not grope,
  But be, from Kent to Cumberland,
At home as on his Hudson slope
  Or Rip Van Winkle's slumberland.

II

How shall you know him ?—by what word,
  What shibboleth, what mole-ridge ?—
Him who will find an English bird
  Just by a line of Coleridge ?

Of outward mark the quickest test
  Is that he wears the shading
That sober Autumn loves the best—
  Soft gray through iron fading.

Tinged, too, are beard and hair; and keen
  His eye, but warm and witty;
A rustic strength is in his mien,
  Made mild by love and pity.

A man of grave, of jolly moods,
  That with the world has kept tune —
You 'd call him Druid in the woods,
  And in the billows Neptune.

Another sign that will not fail:
  Where'er he chance to tarry,—
In copse, or glen, or velvet vale,
  Or where the streamlets marry,

            .

Or on the peaks whose shadows spread
  O'er Grasmere's level reaches,—
You 'll note shy shakings of his head
  Before his Saxon speeches.

III

Ah me! by how poor facts and few
  A stranger may detect us,
While friends may never find the clew,
  Though keenly they inspect us.

Of things that make the *man*—alack!
  I 've hardly even hinted;
We speak of them—behind his back,
  But here?—this might be printed.

Still . . . he 'd not know the portrait his—
  His modesty so blinds him—
But no! . . . to learn what Burroughs *is*
  Shall be his fee who finds him.

www.ingramcontent.com/pod-product-compliance
Lightning Source LLC
Chambersburg PA
CBHW031442270326
41930CB00007B/827